THE PAIN THAT PUSHED ME

THE
PAIN THAT PUSHED ME

J.K. GOODSON

The Pain that Pushed Me

Copyright © 2021 by Jeffrey K. Goodson. All rights reserved.

No part of this publication may be reproduced, stored in a retrieval system or transmitted in any way by any means, electronic, mechanical, photocopy, recording or otherwise without the prior permission of the author except as provided by USA copyright law.

The opinions expressed by the author are not necessarily those of URLink Print and Media.

1603 Capitol Ave., Suite 310 Cheyenne, Wyoming USA 82001
1-888-980-6523 | admin@urlinkpublishing.com

URLink Print and Media is committed to excellence in the publishing industry.

Book design copyright © 2021 by URLink Print and Media. All rights reserved.

Published in the United States of America

Library of Congress Control Number: 2021911000
ISBN 978-1-64753-828-6 (Paperback)
ISBN 978-1-64753-829-3 (Hardback)
ISBN 978-1-64753-830-9 (Digital)

29.06.21

ACKNOWLEDGMENT

I want to dedicate this book to Heavens Elevation, my brother Pastor Jerome Goodson, my HERO!!!

I am so bless to have so many family and friends who often pray for me and support me.

To my wonderful and beautiful wife, Barbara Ann Goodson, you are heaven sent and anointed!

To my son, Alex, I am so proud of you!

To my grand kids!

To my mother, Ruth Goodson, you are my Rock !!

To Chosen Generation cogic, the greatest church on Earth!

To my Bishop VI Prioleau, and keystone jurisdiction family my main man supt Hasan, and Lady Ruth Johnson, love you guys.

To my buddy, Dr. Waverly B Bumbrey ,and that awesome choir refuge temple, Cathedral,VP Supt Herman Hicks .

To my Chairman Bishop Michael B Golden Jr!

To my buddy, Apostle Alexander "bunzy "Thompson, thanks for everything!

To Tamara Oruade and husband Ben thanks for support!

To Pastor Amos Ward and Lady Ward my covenant friends my district missionary mother Denise Marshall!

To Supt Charles Giddens Sr, I'm bless to have so much support.

To Elder Jed Zachary Williams

FORWARD

This book is the story of every man, woman, boy and girl. Regardless of age, gender, Christian, or Non- Christian. Our mind and our heart are both battlegrounds. They are home to many of the pieces of our life experiences that shape us into who we are now. As we all grow older in life, we find ourselves with a mixed bag of emotions and memories.

Some of those experiences carry with them a sweet fragrance, while others have an odor that is unpleasant to even think about. It is those painful incidents that cling like mold at the same time tainting what makes us feel good about ourselves and others around us.

How many times have we heard the English Idiom 'No Pain-No Gain'? It is basically saying, suffering is necessary in order to achieve something.

Jeffrey Goodson (J.K.) shares with us in "The Pain That Pushed Me" whether it be deep-rooted, emotional pain, or a woman giving birth to her baby -pain hurts. Pain can throw you off balance, thwart your plans, and often very hard to quarry. J.K.'s story is one of hope. He encourages us in knowing that no matter what life is throwing at you, or what you are currently walking through, the pain can push you to your Kingdom destiny and divine deliverance.

In connecting and identifying with J.K. it has reminded me that life happens to us all. That you and I at some point in life have to decide what is worth holding onto, and what is detrimental to us if we don't let go of it. Those painful memories that we choose for whatever reason to hold onto, should be fodder for the fuel engine of our success. If not, they will become a chaotic web throughout your life and affect the relationships most dear to you.

What better time for this story to be shared than now. In these times of uncertainty, such as a global pandemic, when millions upon millions are experiencing pain on all fronts of life. We live in a fallen world that keeps us fearfully treading from one crisis to the next. Many in the world at present are feeling helpless, experiencing pain from financial, physical, relational, health, and on distinctive personal levels.

As a result, it is easy to become numb to pain and justify our reaction and make excuses to live with it. However, 'The Pain That Pushed Me' is the good news that you can scrape off the mold and let the pain push you to Kingdom Destiny.

Not to allow the pain life many times will bring to push you, is to give it permission to sit and suffocate your fruit, it rots and becomes an odor.

In this unhealthy state you suffer loss of joy, peace, and happiness.

J.K. encourages you in this read not to let your pain paralyze you, leaving you at a standstill, only wondering what success could have been for you. So, as you read and follow the author as he has been inspired to write 'The Pain That Pushed Me', regardless of your past, don't give pain power to hold you back. Let your pain push you to destiny and let it benefit others as J.K. has done in this book.

He is not asking you to forget the past or be in denial life hasn't hurt and caused you pain, but only asking that you choose how you look at it. Close the door to your pain by forgiving yourself and others, even forgiving what you can't forget.

So, as you walk with J.K. through "The Pain That Pushed Me." You may be in a time and season that is most painful

for you, when you feel like you don't have an ounce of strength, my prayer is, as you read, your head will be lifted so that your eyes can behold something that will bring you hope, and you realize in the end your life and your story matters and get ready to embrace Kingdom destiny. *"You turned my wailing into dancing; you removed my sackcloth and clothed me with joy."* Psalm 30:11

Bishop Jack Vaughn – Kansas City, Kansas

MidAmerica Nazarene University B.A., MSM

INTRODUCTION

She screams in pain while being told to push a little more. The pain grows stronger; she pushes a little harder. She encourages her more. With the pain, she bares the more she pushes. After much coaching and pushing, she delivers a beautiful blessing of joy. Their baby has arrived. Through the sweat and muscle spasms, weight gain, and most of all, the "Pain" she endures through the pain that pushes her.

There will be times when we must go through hard times, uncomfortable situations, sleepless nights, painful conditions when we will conceive our great accomplishments. The pain will push you.

As we navigate the pages of this book, we will talk about painful times that push us to our Kingdom destiny and divine deliverance.

Poverty, sickness, sorrow, trial, and tribulations. But it's a part of life. Two things will come from your deliverance either they will make you or break you.

If you are a child of God, know that it should make you develop you, define you, and deliver you.
Dr. Martin Luther King once said, "you will define a person by not how many times they have fallen but how many times they get back up". There is gain from pain.

Let's begin this journey toward this narrative.
"The pain that pushes you"

CHAPTER 1

THE PAIN HE ENDURED

Isaiah 53:3 But he was wounded for our transgressions, he was bruised for our iniquities: the chastisement of our peace was upon him, and with his stripes, we are healed.

The pain must have been unbearable. Most men would have fainted and collapsed under these conditions and punishments. Not the savior. He died that we might have life.

Verse 3 describes the pain and the agony Jesus endured. He is despised and rejected of men, a man of sorrow and acquainted with grief and we hid as if were our faces from Him. He was despised and we esteemed Him not. Surely he hath borne our griefs and carried our sorrows yet we did esteem Him stricken, smitten of God, and afflicted.

THE PAIN THAT PUSHED ME

Isaiah as only He can gives us a vivid depiction of Jesus Christ. These verses speak of nothing but pain. Go back and read it again. You feel the agony and despair while you are reading such gruesome comments about our savior.

The NIV version gives us a more vivid and detailed depiction of the agony and pain Jesus endured. Here it is: Verse 4 "NIV".
Surely, He took up our infirmities and carried our sorrows, yet we considered Him stricken by God, smitten by Him, and afflicted.

Notice the pain-filled verse where in it goes on to say
He was pierced for our transgressions; He was crushed for our iniquities. The punishment that brought us peace was upon Him and by His wounds, we are healed. My God, Thank you, Jesus.

Look at the pain, agony, and punishment that He endured. But notice where it says; the punishment that brought us peace was upon Him, and by His stripes, we are healed. The pain that pushes us.

What an act of Humility. Jesus took on our pain. Pain pushes Jesus to the cross while we were yet sinners He died for us. I'm trying to keep my composure while writing this chapter.

THE PAIN THAT PUSHED ME

Notice I said, the pain pushes Him to do it for us. Not himself, not God. Again this bare repeating our sins, pain, and transgression push Jesus to the cross. He was wounded for our transgressions! When we encounter pain through our kingdom journey this pain will propel us to your kingdom assignment. Push! Push!

Jesus took our sin, pain, and transgression on the cross so that we would be free. This is a praise moment. Thank you, Jesus, thank you, Jesus, you did it just for me.

In Isaiah 53:5: We have one of the most formidable and powerful verses in the Bible. We must not lose sight of the pain Jesus endured.

Please understand that He is suffering for our transgressions, not punishment, His suffering was given with permission. Notice the plural: our transgressions and our iniquities. This was not a solo act but for all mankind. Isaiah verse 5 KJ shows a personal touch when it affirms our peace was upon Him.

One songwriter declared He was hung up for our hang-ups. This transgression of this iniquity resulted in our deliverance. Another praise God moment.

Verse 5 ends so victoriously and affirms " with His stripes we are healed". The pain He endured resulted in our healing.

THE PAIN THAT PUSHED ME

The pain He endured resulted in our deliverance, the pain He endured resulted in our victory. Again, I repeat by his stripes we are healed.

Some scholars report the number of strikes or lashes was 39. In 2 Corinthians 11:24. Paul talks of receiving 40 lashes less one. Whipping a person 39 times was the standard practice in NT times.

The whips used were made of braided leather, with sharp stones or iron bits attached to the end of the straps. This would tear the flesh of the prisoner, resulting in excruciating pain. The Roman soldiers were trained to inflict this type of cruel and excruciating pain. The beating would also affect the Mental anguish and most of all the spiritual agony of being forsaken for the sins of the world. He cried in agony why has thou forsaken me" He who knew no sin became sin. This was the cruelest of all. Taking our sin! But He did. Can you see it? Can you see it? The pain being pushed.

I shudder while trying to write this paragraph. My hands are shaking. He did this for me! My God, my God.

NOTES

CHAPTER 2

FOR MY SAKE

Matthew 5:11

Bless are ye when men shall revile you, and persecute you and shall say all manner of evil against you falsely (for my sake). When women give birth, she does it for her baby, despite the pain. I must push.

We will suffer the pain of persecutions being taunted ridiculed, scorn, and belittled but we must proceed for His sake. We are given the greatest example, JESUS.

In the great discourse of the beatitudes, He stated that when we suffer these persecutions. We must do it for the sake of the Kingdom and the reward for the pain of the Kingdom. For non-Kingdom people, this beatitude seems liked self-inflicted wounds of pain. But for the Kingdom believers it's knowing that, by His stripes, we are healed. It's knowing that we are more than conquerors, it's knowing

that weeping endures for a night, but joy cometh in the morning.

This reminds us to rejoice and be exceedingly glad, for great is your reward in Heaven. This pain will push you to your Heaven's reward. This mindset of being labeled a pain bearer is developed in your obedience and sacrifice to Jesus Christ. Dr. Martin Luther King once said, "A man isn't fit to live if there's nothing he won't die for".

A pain bearer is one who can allow the pain that they bare to propel and position them to do greater works in the Kingdom. But in order to be a "pain bearer" there must be a sacrificial mindset that qualifies for this label.

A "pain bearer" must understand that their pain will activate the faith that you will need to move forward with a clear understanding of the scriptures.
KJV

Romans 5:3-4
And not only so, but we glory in tribulations. Also knowing that tribulation worketh patience; And patience, experience; and experience, hope.
How's this scripture Roman 8:18 For I reckon that the sufferings of His present time are not worthy to be compared with the glory which shall be revealed in us.

Does every Christian suffer?

CHAPTER 3

POSITION FROM THE PAIN

As we continue to this journey, often when we experience the pain we find ourselves taking a position that was produced from the pain.

I'm reminded when I was a little boy, I had experienced a ruptured appendix. You talking about pain. Oh my God! I found myself bent over, holding my side in agony. The pain I experienced forced me into that position. That's what happens when you are in pain.

As we experience a relationship with the God of Heaven, we grow to rely on Him in every situation we experienced. When it comes to the pain, we are writing about it will place you in a position that will push you to do great things for the Kingdom.

When that woman is giving birth, she's in a position that produces her baby. Is that what God will do for us? He allows the pain we suffer to place us in a position to birth something awesome and bless. Because of our continued relationship with Jesus Christ, we learn to depend on Him to coach us through our struggles, because he knows how to bring us out of the pain and putting us in a position for greatness and growth.

We might bend over in pain, but we are reminded by the Holy Spirit that the pain is putting us in a position to produce for the Kingdom. Know that it's in you, and you will deliver through the pain.

When a pearl is birthed, it began as something that is a hard glistening object. This object is produced within the soft tissue of a living shelled oyster. It secretes grain substance over the mass, which spits out a pearl. From the pain, it produces a pearl.

When we rely on the Holy Spirit, it will help and prepare us when we develop the pain to produce.

Pain is never celebrated or welcome, but we all experience it. I'm not asking you to seek after pain. I'm just trying to help you to flip it and find strength and creation from it.

I was told of a true story about Thomas Edison, who conducted countless experiments with countless kinds of materials often during his work. If the material was found useless, he tosses it out the window. This would cause a pile-up of failures that reach the second story of his house. Now once you are in a position, you are in from the pain. Either you can stay in that position or get up and try to find help. This applies spiritually once you experience pain, you can just stay in that position or rise and do something. In the Bible, there's a story about a woman with a blood problem in Luke 8:41. She suffered from this condition for 12 years. The text does not offer us the exact condition she suffered, but it does affirm that she was declared unclean according to the law. Because of this condition, Luke records that she tried doctors, but to no avail.

Because of the nature of her condition, she endured emotional pain as well. We will discuss her emotions in a later chapter because it was a blood issue this cause a social and religious problem. Anyone who came into contact with her would be considered unclean. This pain put her in a position of rejection, resentment, and remorse.

But despite these challenges she suffered, she didn't throw in the towel. She did not abandon her faith.

So many times the emotion of pain can cause one to just give up and die. But this woman who the Bible does not give a name but legend says her name was a Veronica. But

the Bible refers to her by her condition, "the woman with the issue of blood". She does not give up. She declares by Faith, if I can just touch the hem of His garment, I'll be made whole, St. Luke affirms in chapter 8 verse 43, If I can touch the hem or border of His garment, notice she wasn't trying for His attention or the tassels of His garment she felt that if she could just touch the hem, that's all I need. Just the hem. I'll be clean, now that's real faith. This painful condition pushes her to Jesus. Despite past failures, she trusted Jesus. Some people have conditions that cause them to be bent over or walk with a limp. Pain can cause you to double over. In this Kingdom journey, we will at times double over from this pain. But know that the God of Heaven can heal you.

This pain caused this woman to be weak, that even in her weakest moment she was able to find enough strength to touch the hem of His garments. All I can say is God is able. Whatever the pain you're going through know that God is can heal you.

NOTES

CHAPTER 4

THE MENTAL PAIN

Often what leads to the physical challenge is the stress we take on mentally. It has been documented that the stress we take on often promotes physical pain. The Bible affirms I will give you peace whose mind is stayed on me (Jesus).

Stressing simply means we are not trusting Jesus. We have taken the situation on ourselves but we must allow the mental anguish to activate our faith in God. There's a scripture in the word of God that directs to trust Jesus.

Lean not on thy understanding, and He will direct the path. If there's any sick among you, call for the elders of the church that they will pray the prayer of faith.

The mental pain can be just as devastating as the physical.

The mental challenge can be often confused and hidden. The enemy plays on this. This mental pain. David endured many mental challenges on his journey. In Psalms 88 Verse 1, he writes, I cried day and night before thee. He affirms in verse 15, I am afflicted and ready to die. He also writes in Psalms 142 verse 7, bring my soul out of prison that I may praise they name KJV.

Even with the mental challenge, you can be an overcomer. Now the mental pain can be a demonic attack. In the book of 1 Samuel Chapter 18, Verse 17-23.

King Saul is tormented by an evil spirit. David would then play his harp which would bring relief to King Saul. Music can help push that pain away.

I come to understand in my anguish and despair that when I would begin to praise the God of Heaven and worship Him all the mental pain was forgotten. Praise will push the pain.

So when you are challenged by those foul spirits whip up a persistent praise and watch it free your mind.

Our mental situations are overcrowded with people who have fallen mentally, but the God of Heaven gives us deliverance and confidence in the word of God.

The Bible affirms I will give you perfect peace whose mind is stayed on Jesus.

NOTES

CHAPTER 5

JOB: MR. PAIN

The Bible declared weeping endure for a night, but joy cometh on the morning. This was a scripture that I could never grasp until I read, Mr. Pain himself JOB.
The theme of JOB. Is the suffering of the Godly and the the sovereignty of God?

If there was a visual picture of pain and suffering it would be Mr. JOB himself. Pain has a way of coming out of nowhere when we least expect it. Pain comes interrupting things.
Pain can be even more painful when things are blessed. Well, that's the place JOB was at in this narrative. JOB's life was a place of blessings, wealth, and children. He had it all and at moments twitch lost it all, had it all, lost it all.

You know anyone that had it all, and at a moment blink lost everything. Now JOB lost everything gradually.

THE PAIN THAT PUSHED ME

First of all, a conversation took place between the devil and God. One of few times that an actual conversation was recorded between the God of Heaven and the devil himself. Gradual pain both mentally and physically can be relentless and extreme. One messenger reports, lost after Lost just when it seems the season is over. A disappointment is over, here comes yet another messenger with more gut-wrenching news.

He's losing everything and with no help from his wife and friends. The pain of loneliness sets in. We talked about the mental pain in the presiding chapters. No one to talk to about what he's going through. Then comes a painful situation. He is stricken with a skin disease that saturates his body. JOB can't take a bath because the skin peels off his body. The pain is overwhelming, and he at times feels his faith slipping away.

The pain pushes JOB to reach way down in depths of his faith and JOB won't give up. See, the pain will push you down or up in your Kingdom journey. See our faith is not activating from the mountain top were in but it's activated from the valleys we fall into.

Pain now becomes the calling card, the God of Heaven. C.S. Lewis once said, God whispers to us in our joys, speaks to us about our difficulties and shouts to us in our pain.

NOTES

CHAPTER 6

THE PAIN OF WAITING

JOB has now reached the apex of pain. Just like that everything is gone. JOB has been stripped of his wealth, his family, and his health. Now if that isn't the face of pain and to add insult to injury know pun intended, his friends sit in silence for 7 days.

Then when they decide to talk they accused him of sinning which brought on his suffering and pain. Wow, some kind of friends.

So JOB finds himself amid a life-changing place of pain, brokenness, and suffering. I often say this, that pain will either make or break you. Have you ever been to that place where your faith is being challenged? The pain is relentless. You question your kingdom walk.

THE PAIN THAT PUSHED ME

When you feel the pain overwhelming. You are now in position for God to show up and heal you.
Pain summons the God of Heaven.

Something down in the lower regions of your soul began to push you. You can't even describe it but the pain is pushing you to Jesus Christ, the great healer, the pain bearer. You thought it was unshakeable and unmovable.

But wait, listen to the words from 2 Corinthians verse 12 where it says, for when I am weak, then I am strong.

Our strength that is pushing you comes from the one who bore our sins "Jesus". I just love saying his name. He took our pain. By His stripes, we are healed.

JOB was determined to hold on. He was tried, tested, and tempted. But he would not give up on God. He's being push and push.

When you honestly follow Jesus, when you give your life and make Jesus your savior, something within you is developed and when pain shows up it's activated and it pushing you toward your healing.

How does my weakness provide strength? Only when you experience this can you really understand this. Because of your faith in Jesus, because he took our pain, we experience

His strength. His strength is activated from our weakness, pain, and suffering.

The Bible affirms by His stripes we are healed. Can you see it? While on the cross, He bore our sorrows, our weakness, our pain but He brings healing.

We can look at that scripture again. What a gem! What a scripture! That gives us so much truth, healing, and deliverance. I called it the "pain deliverance scripture". He was wounded for our transgression.

NOTES

CHAPTER 7

PAIN ON THE CROSS

He did it for us! Wow for us! My name was on His list. Thank you Jesus for including me on that list. His pain brings our healing. His stripes bring our strength; His pain brings our gain. His tribulation brings our salvation. Come on say it like this wounded, bruised, wounded, bruised. All this pain pushes me to my salvation. All his pain activated my healing. It says it right there in verse 5. By His stripes, we are healed.
Yes, the pain scripture. Notice it says with His stripes. His stripes. Just say it... His stripes. His stripes bring our healing.

The pain scripture.

Pain from the cross

The experience of pain or loss can be a motivating force.

THE PAIN THAT PUSHED ME

Pain can be a motivating force that will push us to the apex of victory. Tyler Perry suffered the pain of complete loss until he had to sleep in his car. This pain of sacrifice led to his life of riches.

When we look at the cross. We see a bloodstain tree. He sees nothing but pain. The pain of our Lord and savior. Beaten beyond recognition. We see the pain of the mental. We see the pain of abandonment, why thou has forsaken me. We see the physical pain of nails trust into his flesh. Bloodshed on a cross.

E. Stanley Jones once said, at the cross, God wraps His heart in flesh and blood and let it be nailed to the cross for our redemption.

His pain and agony brought our redemption and joy. The songwriter pens the song, what can wash away our sins, nothing but the blood.

But His pain gave us salvation. World-famous surgeon, Paul, brand shares that pain is vital to our bodies. It tells us what is wrong. He learned while in India that pain can be borne with Dignity and a calm spirit. He stated it was there he began treating Leprosy. From the silence of physical pain. The Disfigurement associated with the disease we know has to do with Mummy's sensation of pain. Those with Leprosy lacks an internal system to warn them of

danger and they often wear their fingers, hands, and feet. Down to stumps.

This is what drives us to our source of healing and comfort, Jesus Christ.

Pain that prepares.

How often do you look at pain as preparation? The scripture affirms weeping endures for a night, and joy comes in the morning. The pain of disappointment and suffering often prepares us for what was promised. We just have to endure the pain. While we are trying to navigate the pain we can prepare for the morning.

The Bible talks about an old testament story of a man name Joseph. Joseph had a lot of brothers who began to dislike him because of the dream and favor he received from God and His Father.

The mental pain of being hated by his own brothers had to be devastating to him. This was just the beginning of the painful journey that began in Joseph's life.

Joseph then was left for dead and then sold into slavery more pain than lied on by Potiphar's wife and thrown right back into jail. As we stated in the presiding chapters, this type of mental pain can often lead to a mental breakdown

and even a stroke. But our faith is then activated. Joseph's faith was unlike anyone else in the Bible. Just like Job his faith prevented him from the pain of a mental breakdown but pushed him. Remember he was separated from his father, mother, and all his siblings. He's all alone, no friends abandon by his brothers.

As we reach the close of this journey "The pain that push me" The great teacher professor C S Lewis once said "God whispers to us in our joys, speaks to us in our difficulties and shouts to us in our PAIN
The Bible quotes in Psalms 119,71 it is good for me that I was afflicted
That I might learn your statues

We do not promote PAIN and seek it out, but because of our faith in the GOD of Heaven through Jesus Christ we learn to embrace it because it activates our faith in Jesus and agitates our strength. Many of us would not have known our salvation in Jesus if not for the PAIN THAT PUSH US. I pray that this book on the PAIN THAT PUSHES YOU will elevate your faith and push you to your kingdom assignment and allow the PAIN you experience in your life become a stepping stone

Let the words in 2 Corinthians 12:10 resonates in your soul and give you joy where it declares when I am weak rather than am I strong.

Your PAIN will put you in a position to experience the victory and healing of Jesus Christ.

Shalom

NOTES

www.ingramcontent.com/pod-product-compliance
Lightning Source LLC
LaVergne TN
LVHW021735060526
838200LV00052B/3298